Bi...

Coloring Book

Lisa Bonforte

Dover Publications, Inc.
New York

Copyright © 1992 by Lisa Bonforte.
All rights reserved under Pan American and International
Copyright Conventions.

Published in Canada by General Publishing Company, Ltd.,
30 Lesmill Road, Don Mills, Toronto, Ontario.

Birds Coloring Book is a new work, first published by Dover
Publications, Inc., in 1992.

International Standard Book Number: 0-486-27356-3

Manufactured in the United States of America
Dover Publications, Inc., 31 East 2nd Street, Mineola, N.Y.
11501

Note

Here is a collection of interesting birds for you to color. Some of them, like the robin and the blue jay, you may have seen outside of your window; others, like the great blue heron and the rhinoceros hornbill, may be new to you. All of them will provide hours of fun as you color the birds and learn their names at the same time.

American Kestrel

Bald Eagle

Barn Owl

Barn Swallows

Belted Kingfisher

Black Skimmer

9

Blue Jay

Brown Pelican

Brown Thrasher

California Quail

Canada Goose

Cardinal

Cedar Waxwing

Chickadee

Chicken—Hen

Chicken—Rooster

Crows

Downy Woodpecker

Eastern Bluebird

Eastern Meadowlark

Flamingo

Goldfinch

Great Blue Heron

Great Cormorant

Great Horned Owl

Herring Gulls

House Wren

Hummingbird

Killdeer

Mallard Duck

Mockingbird

Mute Swan

Northern Flicker

Northern Oriole

37

Ostrich

Parakeets

Parrot

Penguin

Pigeons

Puffin

Red-breasted Nuthatch

Redwing Blackbird

Rhinoceros Hornbill

Ring-necked Pheasant

Roadrunner

Robin

Rose-breasted Grosbeak

Roseate Spoonbill

Ruffed Grouse

Screech Owl

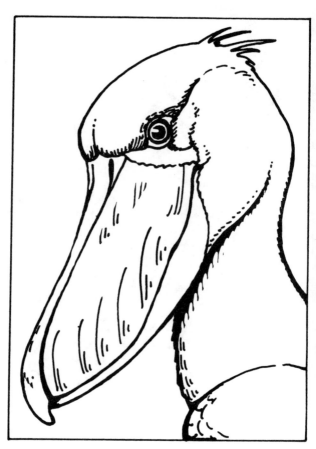

Shoebill Stork

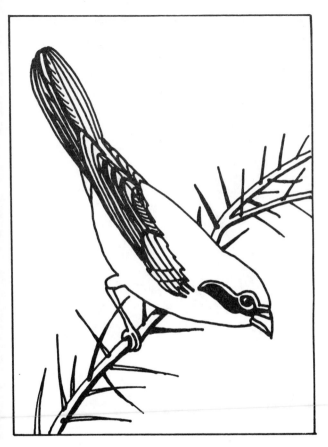

Shrike

Snowy Egret

Toucan

Tufted Titmouse

Turkey

Turkey Vultures

White Stork

White-throated Sparrow

Wood Duck